I0490709

MAKE MONEY ON INVESTMENTS:

The Benefits & The Risks Of Investing In

Hedge Funds

DAN WILSON

TABLE OF CONTENTS

INTRODUCTION

A hedge fund is an official investment venture that pools money together, to be managed by professional management firms. Hedge fund operations given this common purpose, are distinctly different from mutual funds. Hedge funds are less limited relative to mutual funds, have more stringent minimum investment requirements, follow strategies that are more versatile and potentially risky, and function with far less transparency.

The hedge funds investment aim is to maximize returns, but to accomplish this objective, management companies use different strategies. While not all of them have the same criteria as other securities, hedge funds still have a prospectus, called the "offering report," outlining the fund's specific strategy, including leverage caps.

Because of their distinctive fee structures, many of

the most accomplished portfolio managers aim to work for hedge funds. Management fees are not only higher than those for mutual funds, but hedge funds also include additional fees that are not paid by mutual funds. Incentive fees based on earned profits can vary from 10% to 30%, although higher fees have been agreed. Hedge fund investors expect their managers to make very large returns and often allow recovery of any losses incurred before future profits are counted against incentive fees.

Hedge funds pool investors ' capital and invest in bonds or other forms of assets in order to achieve positive returns. Hedge funds (HF) are not regulated as strictly as mutual funds and typically have more leeway to follow investments and strategies that may increase the risk of investment losses than mutual funds. Hedge funds are limited to wealthy investors who are able to afford the higher fees and risks of investing in hedge funds and institutional investors, including pension funds.

WHAT ARE THE FUNDS FOR HEDGE?

A hedge fund operates like a mutual fund, but it does not have the same limitations on how investors can spend capital from the account. Investors can not easily buy or sell shares in a hedge fund as opposed to a mutual fund. Hedge funds are usually open-ended and require monthly or quarterly additional contributions or withdrawals.

Hedge funds can invest in almost any asset class, including risky short-sales, real estate, bonds, buying and selling whole businesses, or following a particular investment theory or guideline. Many members of the Billionaire Group, including George Soros, David Einhorn, Bill Ackman, John Paulson, and some others, made their money as hedge fund managers.

In general, hedge funds are limited to wealthy

investors with an appetite for high risks and high fees, unlike public mutual funds. Typical fees for hedge funds include a management fee of 2 percent and a performance fee, typically around 20 percent, Being paid to the manager over the previous year for investment gains. For charges like that, it's no wonder that the hedge fund industry has so many billionaires!

Most of the hedge funds currently available are typically organized as a partnership, where the general partner is the director of the portfolio. It is this partner that will make the hedge fund investment decisions, while the rest of the partners in the partnership is the ones who make the investment. This financial market has almost as little regulation and regulatory constraints as similar securities, such as mutual funds, have.

The general partner, as the hedge fund portfolio manager, seeks to achieve targeted returns or absolute results from the investments they make, irrespective of how the rest of the financial market is doing. As previously mentioned, these individuals will use several different techniques or approaches to help them achieve their goals. While some tend to use investment strategies for equity, fixed-income, or CTA, there are some hedge fund managers who prefer to use maths algorithms to make their investors the right kind of returns.

Like any other type of investment, hedge fund managers are subject to the same financial rules and regulations as other traders are. When it comes to the techniques they use, though, you will find that these forms are not so easily accessible to others who handle controlled securities such as mutual funds, so there is a greater amount of risk to a person's investment, although the benefits are also higher.

To obtain a complete return on their investment by a hedge fund manager, they need to be versatile. As mentioned earlier, some different methods and techniques need to be implemented and integrated to achieve the above.

HEDGE FUND STRUCTURE.

Many hedge funds are organized as limited partnerships, and there are a couple of key players to the community.

Investors: Individuals investing in a hedge fund must be either an accredited investor (annual income of $200,000 or more) or a high-net worth individual (net worth more than $1 million).

Investment Manager: An investment manager makes a lot of hedge fund decisions, including where to allocate capital and manage the risk.

Prime broker: A special category of broker that will assist the fund in executing large investment transactions.

Executing broker: The executing broker is responsible for carrying out and distributing the transactions of the hedge fund. They will ensure that everything complies with their applicable policies and procedures.

PROFITS IN HEDGE FUND INVESTING

Some people understand what a mutual fund is and conclude that the same thing is a hedge fund investment. We're correct in that, like a mutual fund, a hedge fund is a group of investors pooling their money. Nevertheless, hedge funds do not have the same kind of regulation the mutual fund does. In reality, to invest in a hedge fund and a certain amount of investment savvy, you should have a certain amount of wealth. The investment in a hedge fund is not a public offering, but often a limited private venture with the fund manager as the general partner.

Hedge funds do this because it is a private investment that can not be achieved by conventional mutual funds. The ability to sell short is one example. This is especially a dangerous strategy if it is a naked short sale. The short sale is when you sell a stock in hopes of buying it later to fill the inventory at a cheaper price.

A naked sale is one where you are selling a non-owned stock. You must be able to borrow it from someone before you sell it in compliance with government regulations. The reason it's so risky because after you sell the stock, the price may spike. So you have to pay huge amounts to satisfy your seller obligations.

When major hedge funds use the tactics, they often deliberately push down the price of stock sales, and minutes later, they will make a quick profit by purchasing and distributing the cheaper stock. This is one way a portfolio of hedge funds provides more income than the average mutual fund.

A hedge fund's original purpose was to protect against the fluctuations of the market. The mixture of different types of investment offered a buffer against falling markets. The change came as it became more common for hedge funds. Today, they provide not only a buffer against loss, but also a benefit advantage.

The standard investment in the hedge fund includes derivatives that are high yields and liabilities from companies that are considered risks, so they have to pay more to borrow or sell their loans at discounted rates, which means higher returns. This is a good comfortable return if you use a $1,000 loan as an example, with the company loan rate at 8 percent. So, if the same company gets back on the panics of the mortgage and the lending institution, they might sell it to the hedge fund at a 50% reduction in the balance. It means that the fund not only collects 16 percent interest but that if the company actually pays the loan in full, they make a 100 percent return on the money.

If you already have a lot of money, you might be the perfect candidate for an investment in a hedge fund. These types of investments are in addition to normal investments. We try to defeat bear markets and bring in money while taking advantage of the bull market and delivering higher returns as well. There are risks in a hedge fund that would never be taken by the average investor. The short-selling technique is one of the best ways to hedge the bad market and take the lemon that the economy has given you and make lemonade with the onset of a bear market.

KEY HEDGE FUND CHARACTERISTICS.

Hedge funds have several key features that distinguish them from other types of pooled investments like mutual funds. The most striking difference is their minimal investment choice.

Often Employ Leverage.

Hedge funds will often use debt or borrowed money to boost their returns, potentially exposing them to a much wider range of investment. Because of increased exposure to collateralized debt and high leverage rates, hedge funds were particularly hard hit in the subprime crisis that kicked off the recession.

Wider Investment Latitude.

The investment universe of a hedge fund is constrained only by its mandate. Essentially, a hedge fund can invest in anything–land, properties,

13

derivatives, currencies, and other alternative resources.

Structure Of Fees.

Rather than paying only a ratio of expenses, hedge funds charge both a ratio of expenses and a fee for results. The standard fee structure is called "Two and Twenty" (or "2 and 20"): a fee of 2 percent for the management of capital and then a 20 percent reduction in any gains.

PROS AND CONS OF HEDGE FUNDS INVESTMENT.

Pros of Hedge Funds.

Hedge funds should be obvious to deliver some important advantages over traditional investment funds. Several notable advantages of hedge funds include:

Aggressive strategy for investment.

When it comes to hedge funds, one thing is particularly clear: investment aggressiveness.

To realize the higher return, this is necessary. These investment strategies also include short selling, using borrowed money to purchase more[leverage purchase] assets and eventually derivatives.

Long or short Selling Of hedge fund.

This is one of the utilized strategies that hedge fund managers approaches. They can either buy the stocks that they feel are undervalued or sell the stocks that they consider undervalued in the same case. It is easier to remember, however, that funds will be exposed to the equity market in a positive way.

Leverage Strategy.

The creditors will borrow and sell money in addition to the equity they would receive in a leveraging strategy. The strategy's advantage is that it can boost returns.

Anticipation for a huge gain, however, is a hedge against the risk of huge loss. Therefore, if this technique is to be used by hedge fund managers, then advanced risk management techniques should be in place.

Flexibility.

The hedge funds are much more versatile than the mutual funds.

SEC[Securities and Exchange Commissions] put no focus on hedge funds. Essentially, people are not freely selling hedge funds. For this reason, they are more versatile since their quality is not controlled by any particular body.

A hedge fund could use techniques to invest across a variety of investment opportunities, such as short selling, derivatives, and leverage.

Short selling (shorting) is one of the key elements to look at. Short selling (shorting) in finance is a way to take advantage of declining security, bond or stock prices. This is a contract dimension to what most investors would like. Benefit from their investment option's rising price.

Lose Reduction.

A hedge fund that delivers consistent returns in many instances increases the value of the portfolio. This is in case of dropping or underperforming all the conventional investments. There are some good returns with the fixed-income-volatility hedge fund strategies.

The hedge funds will reduce the losses during share market sell-offs.

For example, if there is a sell-off on the market, which is somewhat volatile, the risk of failure can be reduced significantly, and even by nearly 80%. Unlike traditional investments, where there are 100% risks of failure.

With the hedge funds ' risk management plan, the shareholder could increase their portfolio by more than 50 percent. Compared to other sites for investment, this is unusual.

Expert Advice And Transparency.

Hedge funds are one of the funds giving their staff beautiful salaries. Apart from being experienced in investment-related matters, the hedge fund managers are also well versed in financial management problems.

Therefore, as an investor, you are guaranteed to get the best information when you go to the market — advice on which to use the hedge funds. In the quality of individual funds, too, future projections.

Their disclosure is one aspect that attracts investors to hedge funds. We don't need any public trade. Investors and regulators are practically unable to control the actions of managers of the fund

Diversification.

There are some reasons why hedge funds should be included in an investment portfolio. The fund's ability to add diversification and reduce risk is one of the most important and fundamental factors.

Hedge funds have the potential to diversify the portfolio by providing a wide range of investments. Some of the opportunities managers take are the long/short, strategic trading, event-driven and also the emerging markets.

The managers can reduce the risks by taking advantage of this diversification potential. In a specific style, though. Hedge funds allow investors to quickly diversify into an investment portfolio. This is especially beneficial for investors with a larger pool of portfolios of hedge funds, but too small to achieve proper diversification.

Cons Of Hedge Funds.

Of course, hedge funds have risk as well:

Downside Capture

This is a risk management tool used to determine what degree of correlation a hedge has with a particular market. It occurs with the hedge funds demanding/claiming targets for absolute returns.

The lower the capture of the downside, the better the fund can retain capital during any recession in the economy.

The optimal correlation with the economy happens when there is a 100% formula. The downside of this is that all the funds available are aligned with a single sector index.

Hedge Fund Fees The majority of hedge funds running have a fee structure commonly known as "2 and 20."

What normally happens in the system is that investors pay a management fee of 2 percent. Generally this fee is for the fund's activities. In contrast, the fund manager must also be paid 20 percent. Typically this is a performance fee to fund the manager for any year-round income.

Sounds familiar?

Considering an investment vehicle such as mutual funds. These often have management fees below 2% in mutual funds. There's no performance fee on top of that. The high fees mean that a hedge fund's investment growth needs to be sufficiently large. This is to outweigh the status quo of results.

Let's not forget: this means more opportunity of better performance in hedge fund investing.

This is the basis of the management and the quality fee. This results in more risk-taking by the manager to increase the performance and therefore, a nicer return. This could be huge losses that would drive the investors away from the company.

The Risks And Returns

The Hedge Funds are seen as an investment vehicle that takes on so many risks.

They usually drag so many risks with them in their investment strategies in pursuit of a larger return (SEC report). The higher risk could result in a return failure. The problem is double-edged, however, in this situation. It can be a boom, and it can be a bust as well.

Throughout 2011, with a 4.8 percent loss, the hedge funds dropped below the index. As the other equivalent (mutual funds) performed reasonably well, this was quite disappointing.

Standard Deviation Hedge funds use this analytical method to estimate the risk of investing in a particular fund.

By taking a closer look at it: if a certain fund has an average annual return of say 8% and the standard deviation is about 3%. An investor would then expect a return of between 5% and 11%. 68% of the time (a standard deviation from the average 8%-3% and also 8% + 3%).

The buyer would be expected to be between 2% and 14% in the same situation. 95% of the time (two standard deviations from the median 8%-6% and also 8% + 6%).

TYPES OF HEDGE FUNDS

Hedge funds may follow a variety of strategies, including macro, debt, relative value, securities in distress, and activism. A macro-hedge fund invests in shares, bonds and currencies in the expectation of benefiting from shifts in macro-economic variables such as global interest rates and countries ' economic policies. An equity hedge fund can be global or country-specific, investing in attractive stocks while hedging shortages of overvalued stocks or stock indices against downturns in equity markets. A hedge fund of relative value benefits from price or spreads inefficiencies. Certain tactics for hedge funds include aggressive growth, sales, emerging markets, value, and short selling.

The "fund of funds" approach is another popular strategy that a hedge fund mixes other pooled investment vehicles and matches other hedge funds. The combination of different strategies and asset classes was designed to deliver a more sustainable long-term return on investment than any of the individual funds. The combination of underlying strategies and funds will monitor returns, risk, and volatility.

Notable Hedge Funds.

Today, the Paulson Funds, a group of independent hedge funds founded by John Paulson, are included in prominent hedge funds. When his fund earned billions from betting against mortgages in 2008, Paulson became popular. Paulson has other unique hedge funds, including one that, for instance, invests primarily in gold.

Pershing Square is a highly successful hedge fund run by Bill Ackman, a high-profile investor. Ackman invests in businesses, he feels undervalued in order to take a more active role in extracting value in the business. Usually, activist tactics include replacing the board of directors, hiring new managers or forcing the company to sell. Also very active activist hedge funds are led by Carl Icahn, a well-known activist. In fact, one of its holding companies, Icahn Enterprises (IEP), is traded publicly and provides an opportunity for investors who are unable or unwilling to invest directly in a hedge fund to bet on Icahn's ability to unlock value.

Regulation Of Hedge Funds.

Another unique characteristic of hedge funds: they face little Securities and Exchange Commission oversight, particularly in comparison with mutual funds, pension funds, and other investment vehicles. That's because hedge funds are primarily taking money from those "professional" or approved investors, high-net worth individuals who meet the above-mentioned net worth criteria. While some funds work with non-accredited investors; U.S. securities laws dictate that at least a plurality of participants in the hedge fund are qualified. The SEC considers them sufficiently sophisticated and affluent to understand and manage the potential risks arising from the wider investment mandate and strategies of a hedge fund, and therefore does not subject the funds to the same regulatory oversight.

But don't make a mistake, hedge funds are limited and they've been getting more and more under the microscope lately. Hedge funds have become so large and powerful (thousands of hedge funds are currently operating by most reports, collectively managing over $1 trillion) that the SEC is beginning to pay more attention. Yet infringements such as insider trading tend to occur much more often, something authorities are coming down hard on.

STRATEGIES OF HEDGE FUNDS.

While the characteristics mentioned above are shared by all hedge funds, they may approach earning money differently. Before we go into hedge fund management strategies, there are two words you need to use.

Long trade: an asset hoped by a trader will increase in price.

Short trade: a trader's expectations for an asset can fall in price.

Long / Short Equity

A hedge fund strategy for long / short equity is very easy. Investors buy price-increasing equities and sell those that are likely to decrease in value. A long trade and a short exchange. With two companies in the same industry, it is common for investors to do this: invest in a predicted winner and loser. The winner's cash gains can be used to help the losers. The fund will see a profit either way if it is done correctly.

Convertible Arbitrage.

A convertible hedge fund for arbitration is long on convertible bonds, or securities that can be exchanged into stocks, and short on shares that can be converted into convertible bonds. This approach seeks to take advantage of the inefficiencies of the convertible bonds of a company.

Fixed-Income Arbitrage.

The technique of fixed-income arbitrage is a strategy in which the hedge fund invests in both sides of a competitive conflict to compensate for small price differences. These hedge funds, including government bonds, will keep an eye on fixed-income returns. They take a long and short stance, often with leverage, when they experience mispricing, and then see a gain when the price is set on the market.

Market Neutral.

The neutral market strategy places equal value on the market's short and long trades. Get it? They are neutral to the market's current conditions. Investors balance the short and long stock positions they take. So they win either way if one ends up doing better than the other.

Credit.

Another example of a fund that invests in other businesses' debt is a credit hedge fund. Investing in a hedge fund focused on credit requires a lot of knowledge in the capital structure's debt side.

Global Macro.

In an attempt to profit from the impact of political or economic developments on a particular market, international macro hedge funds invest in stocks, bonds and currencies. This process involves in-depth assessments of a nation's economy's rise and decline. They put themselves to benefit from an economic or political event's particular outcome.

Merger Arbitrage.

Arbitration strategies are attempting to manipulate price differences between closely related assets. Using financial leverage is often involved in the process.

An investor will take opposing sides in two companies that are actually combining a merger arbitrage. Before the transaction takes place, the stock is bought and the buyer expects a return once it is completed. We must remember, however, bear in mind the fact that the merger may not be completed on time or at all.

Event-Driven

An event-driven strategy involves hedge funds buying stock as stocks are inflating and deflating after a case, such as a merger or bankruptcy. Such funds will sometimes buy the debt of businesses in financial distress or bankrupt. We must buy senior debt first, because it is the cash that must first be paid back by failed companies.

Short Only.

The only short path is simply seeking to discover accounting fraud or any misrepresentation of stock value in a financial statement.

HOW TO CHOOSE THE RIGHT HEDGE FUND.

Hedge funds provide an enticing alternative to traditional investment methods, and it is important to optimize your returns to choose the correct fund. Because so many different types and styles of hedge funds are available, it may seem like a daunting or tedious process to choose the right one. There are a few simple concepts, however, that will help you narrow your choices when it comes to your own investment strategy for hedge funds. You want to understand the types of investments, the methods used to administer the fund, the fund manager's expertise and, last but not least, the words that govern the fund and your investment.

Even though this is your first such fund purchase, you have certainly invested in other kinds of securities, shares and/or bonds. The important first step is to understand how these basic types of investment work. Because many hedge funds invest in both conventional and non-traditional sources, you will want to understand how these types of traditional investment strategies are influenced by the economy. Find out what types of investments the hedge fund will focus on and use this information to determine whether or not there is a solid basis for the underlying strategies of the fund.

Strategies for the investment fund can and do vary widely. Make sure you clarify the forms of hedging techniques and how they will be used and in what circumstances they will be used when speaking to the fund manager. Many types of hedging strategies are more dangerous than others, and when using these strategies, you should consider whether the threat is comparable with the potential gain. Most hedge funds provide information on the types of strategies that are allowed to be used in the fund itself when you are in the consideration process. Compare similar fund approaches to determine the return potential of your initial investment.

The skill of your fund manager is just as critical as the types of investments and strategies. In general, managers of hedge funds are paid based on the performance of the fund. Although large profits are never guaranteed, it ensures that hedge fund managers have an intimate stake in their decisions by binding payment to the fund's results. You're going to want to speak to the hedge fund manager and ask questions about the investing style, his industry knowledge, and his overall investment strategy-make sure you feel comfortable with the answers before moving on with your investment.

Ensure you fully understand the terms of your hedge fund before you take the final move to invest-most of them have a lock-out period during which the investments will be unavailable to you. Make sure this is compatible with other related hedge funds. Always, pay attention to the terms of payouts and liquidity, as well as the charges you are expected to pay. Ideally, your hedge fund manager should also have a substantial amount invested in the fund-this can help curb any potentially risky investments that might result in a large loss.

Overall, selecting the right hedge fund will require a lot of research, careful planning, and even more careful choices once you've made your initial assessment. By choosing a hedge fund that works with investment vehicles you understand, and with a management that has solid, reliable experience, you can make sure your investment has the best chance of making excellent returns.

Consult the Financial Pacific professionals, whether you're a seasoned financial investor or a beginner only starting out in the world of international investment. Have the experience, skills and determination to help you achieve your financial goals. Successful wealth management needs an individualized approach, and with reliable knowledge and rigorous analysis, Financial Pacific provides flexibility and selection.

REASONS WHY YOU CAN TAKE ADVANTAGE OF HEDGE FUNDS.

Typically, hedge fund is the part of the investment portfolio that seeks good returns through active portfolio management. Such funds are usually an investment strategy based on skills that seeks to achieve returns depending on the trader's exclusive ability or rule. The returns earned are called "definite" because they do not depend on the long-term return of simple stock and bond markets. For many factors, investors are intrigued by hedging funds. Hedge funds have the potential to deliver positive returns in all kinds of market conditions, they have a low relation to traditional asset classes, and above all they give way to highly focused targets that are usually not achievable by conventional money management.

The hedge funds are viewed as private investment undertakings and are not widespread with less than 100 investors. Not all hedge funds are appropriate for all potential investors and most of them are marketed to individuals who meet such specific financial criteria. Until investing in hedge funds, it is necessary to determine the appropriateness of the investor with respect to its risk tolerance, investment goals and experience with the portfolio.

There are many ways out of hedge funds to generate income. First of all, hedge funds are a managed pool of investments for institutions or wealthy individual investors which take into account one of the many trading strategies in equities, bonds or derivatives, aiming to benefit from market inadequacy and hedge the underlying risks to some degree. Hedge funds are generally co-ordinated in an unsafe manner and are typically much less visible than conventional investment funds. This feature lets them trade in a hidden way. Generally, hedge funds have short periods of investment, and pay fees that rely on both operational and operating funds. Treating hedge funds under the asset class is a flaw on the part of investors; instead, the investment community treats these funds as a variety of trading approaches. The right decision for an individual investor to hedge policy depends primarily on their portfolio. So if the portfolio is such that it indicates strong equity investment, then the sought-after hedging technique is to offset equity risk. It may be clear by now that the statement of comparative returns between hedge fund strategies can be misleading.

Second, hedge funds use investment strategies that are usually prohibited to sell more traditional investments, such as lending stocks, in hopes of eventually buying them back at a lower price and using big power by borrowing. The preferred plans, however, are likely to change. The word used here is global macro where one invests in international markets shifts, often using spin-offs to understand interest rate or currency changes.

Third by pursuing those tactics, you will reap

considerable income. These include the convertible arbitrage which involves going forward extensively in convertible securities that are stocks or bonds that are then exchanged at a fixed price for a particular number of other types, generally common shares, thus shortening the main shares. This is the past's old and effective strategy, but it now seems to be losing its luster. Another strategy is to invest in emerging markets where, by buying bonds or stocks, one can invest in securities of the growing economies ' companies. Investing in a "Hedge Fund Basket" is another hedge fund. Many funds will concentrate on single strategies here, while others will follow composite strategies. But these funds have a system of high fees. You can remain market neutral where equal amounts of capital are invested in the market long and short with an effort to counteract risk by purchasing undervalued securities and taking shorter place in overvalued securities.

WHAT DO I NEED TO KNOW IF I INTEND TO INVEST IN A HEDGE FUND?

Know these before getting started with Hedge Fund Investment:

- Be a qualified investor: You usually have to be an accredited investor to invest in hedge funds, which means you have a minimum level of income or capital.

- Read the prospectus and documents applicable to a project. Be sure that you understand the level of risk involved in the investment strategies of the fund and that the risks are acceptable for your personal investment goals, time horizons, and sensitivity to risk. The higher the potential returns then the higher the risks you have to assume, as with any investment.

- Understand the valuation of the fund's assets. Hedge funds can hold hard-to-sell and hard-to-value investments. You should grasp the valuation process and know to what degree independent sources valuate investments of a company.

- Understand the fees. Fees have an impact on your investment return. Hedge funds typically charge a 1-2% asset management fee, plus a "performance fee" of 20% of the hedge fund's profit. A performance fee might motivate a manager of a hedge fund to take higher risks in the hope of producing a greater return.

- Understand any limitations on the right to redemption of your shares. Hedge funds typically limit redemption or cash-in opportunities for your shares to four times a year or less, and often impose a one-year or more "lock-up" period during which you can not cash your shares.

- Managers of hedge fund analysis. Be sure hedge fund managers are qualified to manage the money and find out if the investment industry has a disciplinary background.

- You can receive this information by reviewing the Form ADV of the broker, which is the registration form of the investment advisor. You can use the SEC's Investment Adviser Public Disclosure (IAPD) website to scan and access a company's Form ADV.
- If the investment advisor company is not found in the IAPD database of the SEC, call your state securities regulator or search the BrokerCheck database of FINRA.
- Ask questions. You entrust somebody else with your money. You will know where your money will go, who will handle it, how it will be spent and how you can get it back. You may also want to read the investor warning from FINRA, which outlines some of the risks involved with investing in hedge fund funds.

HOW TO START A HEDGE FUND

It is important to understand the financial and legal criteria first if you want to learn how to start a hedge fund. The launching of a hedge fund is not the same method as starting a business because of the risks and capital requirements. Here's the basics of launching a hedge fund you need to learn.

Hedge funds derive their name from the original strategy of using a combination of long and short strategies to "hedge" investor risk. This strategy aims to achieve reasonable returns regardless of the direction in which the stock market moves. Most hedge fund investors are accredited investors, which means they have to meet or exceed the initial investment criteria of net worth and minimum.

Why Start a hedge fund?

Money managers or registered investment advisors who are specialized in hedging strategies typically start hedge funds. They then use these skills and strategies to attract investors and make a profit. As with other products and services, due to market demand, somebody could start a hedge fund. In July 2018, hedge fund assets reached a record level of $3.235 trillion worldwide, according to Hedge Fund Research.

Although risky, hedge funds often attract high-net worth investors, which means assets can grow at a much faster rate than mutual funds or ETFs. This potential for growth also motivates money managers and consultants to start hedge funds. Hedge fund managers can also order high fees, often around 1% to 2% of assets and 20% of earnings above a certain target return.

Steps to Start a Hedge

Fund The hedge fund start-up phase has some parallels with starting a business. Starting a hedge fund, however, is more complex— and increasingly difficult.

Differentiate Between Hedge And Mutual Funds.

They are similar in that a fund manager controls all pools of money. There are several key differences, however, other than this. It is essential to consider these differences when beginning one.

First, hedge funds are not as regulated as mutual funds, so they can invest in a more diverse and risky range of securities and use strategies that can not be used by mutual funds. Hedge funds (HF) can use large amounts of leverage, short sell, and carry out riskier trading on behalf of their investors, while mutual funds can not.

Remember that prior to purchase, the approaches applicable to the hedge fund manager must be listed in the private placement memorandum.

Second, there are different levels of distribution for hedge funds and mutual funds. Mutual funds are publicly traded securities and are open to all investors with SEC-approved prospectuses. Hedge

47

funds are financed by private placements with accredited investors, who must have a net value of more than $1 million (home value not included) or an annual income of more than $200,000 (now and in the future).

Third investors in hedge funds appear to be "locked-in" for a period of time. While a mutual fund investor can sell their shares whenever they want, for a certain period of time a hedge fund shareholder may be restricted.

Finally, managers of hedge funds are paid differently than managers of mutual funds. Mutual fund managers receive a fixed percentage of total assets managed annually, while hedge fund managers typically receive a percentage of total assets (usually around 2 percent), plus a percentage of earned income. Typically, this figure is about 20%.

Manager compensation is specified in the prospectus of the hedge fund and the investor agrees to this.

Basic steps to start a hedge fund are identified here.

Choose A Strategy

Hedge fund managers usually start with a successful investment track record over the years of industry experience. This is how their first customers are drawn and their resources are built up. But even with the required experience, you will also need your fund's overall vision, including an understanding of how it will produce returns for investors. Hedge funds may adopt a number of different strategies, including:

Market Neutral Strategy: This strategy is a popular one, involving purchasing a group of securities that are expected to rise, and then offsetting these investments by short-selling the overall market (for example, one of the S&P 500 Index ETFs). If the portion to go up is better than the portion of the short-sold, the fund will make money. This can be a valuable marketing strategy for investors worried about market crashes.

Global Macro Strategy: This type of strategy aims at making money from major trends in the economy. This could be a good strategy to try if you have comprehensive knowledge of economics, global economic patterns, global economies, and how these elements work together. Global macro strategies make money by creating an idea of what will happen to the (or multiple) levels of a particular country, stock index, interest rate, currency, or inflation / deflation.

Hedged equity strategy: This approach is similar to a market-neutral strategy, except that instead of shortening the entire portion of the portfolio you're expecting to rise on a dollar-for-dollar basis, only one portion would be shortened. For example, if you had a portfolio of $1 million, $300,000 could be shortened. This means there would be some coverage if the market collapsed, but the fund would also be designed to make money from rising stocks.

Usually, hedge fund managers follow a strategy to reduce asset volatility while optimizing the potential for upside gain. In times of anticipated declines in the market, this may mean buying stocks at low speed while shortening safety at high speeds. In this way, greater gains in the latter will offset the loss in the former.

Find Legal Help.

It may be one of the largest start-up costs for hedge funds to hire the right form of lawyer, but it may also be the biggest initial investment. A hedge fund lawyer will help you write key terms, including performance payments, for service agreements with clients. They can also help to properly register the hedge fund with your state or the SEC.

Secure Financing.

Start-up costs for hedge funds can range from $100,000 to $300,000 similar to other types of business, start-up costs depend on a number of factors including building / location, number of staff and legal costs. Financing can come from friends, family, angel investors, banks, and seeders of hedge funds, crowdfunding, or perhaps a small business loan.

Understand The Risks.

You not only bear the risks of business ownership when you own, manage and run a hedge fund, but you also bear market risks, including interest rate, financial, asset, and currency risks.

HEDGE FUND VOLATILITY

The volatility of the Hedge fund is a particularly important topic now with a feeling of uncertainty for the market and economy. The first thing to understand is precisely what a hedge fund is. The hedge fund is a fund that can invest in short-term or long-term investments, but the primary strategy is to remain in stocks for as long as possible to maximize revenue and minimize risk to investors, and to get out before the fund has lost money on that particular investment. These are intended to return to their owners, regardless of what happens on the economy, by protecting their original investment and moving in and out of stocks or bonds until these experience a recession.

Hedge funds are only available to a small number of investors, but they are allowed to invest in a variety of types of things, such as stocks and bonds, debts and assets, and things like real estate that are not related to the regular stock market. A hedge fund pays the manager a fee to run the fund.

The effectiveness between a hedge fund and a typical investor fund is that hedge funds invest in such a wide variety of investment types, and most funds are just an opportunity for investors to do very well. The fund manager also plays a very different role than a mutual fund investor and is exploring all sorts of investment opportunities.

While addressing hedge funds, risk is an interesting concept since hedge funds do not typically face as much uncertainty as the normal market. But at this moment, each fund is experiencing uncertainty, and hedge funds and standard investment funds are suffering from market volatility.

In reality, general market volatility is important for hedge funds because fund managers thrive on the crazy market to be able to invest in stocks at a low point and sell them until they hit the bottom. Good fund managers are able to take advantage of market volatility and use it to increase profits to their benefit.

It is important to be willing to invest in a fund for a reasonable amount of time, because funds are intended to go up and down in value, and it is best to find a fund that takes advantage of the volatility of hedge funds if you intend to invest in hedge funds.

TIPS FROM EXPERT HEDGE FUND MANAGER.

Read on if you're looking to expand your hedge fund start-up business and tips from top hedge fund manager and experts. Hedge fund manager job revolves around creative, unconventional methods of producing unusual outcomes. It's also about keeping business going during a crisis.

Read about the fascinating tips and tricks for hedge fund management to keep you on trading. Also, it can lay the foundation for a stronger startup that will be sufficiently robust to bear market ups and downs.

The Hedge fund startups are a unique investment vehicle, but it's all about predicting and capturing the patterns that drive growth. Bucking the trend is as critical in the financial markets as joining it.

There should be a certain amount of independent thinking that serves as a way to carve a separate path from the herd, irrespective of whether you are in a bull market or bear.

Market swings must be correctly anticipated for the management of strategic hedge funds. This is the key to market success, as this can influence the make or break difference.

The Power of Informed Decisions.

The manager of hedge funds must set realistic goals and important schedules. It can have disastrous consequences to try to start a hedge fund. Take your time to develop effective strategies and choose the best growth service providers.

Hedge fund manager should also create strong shareholder relationships with leading brokers through capital distribution services, as this can help drum up more business. If you're trying to introduce investors to new hedge funds, it's important to participate in the introduction of assets.

Operational Risk Assessment Has Its Rewards New hedge fund manager needs to worry about the operational risk involved in creating hedge funds.

Risk assessment is an essential step forward— the goal should be to find out if the fund's holdings are valued accurately and can be valued during each dealing period. Any valuation risk analysis requires all parties involved in valuing the assets of the company.

Do The Research.

It's important to be ready for homework before you get to class. From the inside out, you need to be informed about the risks involved in the hedge fund industry and have specific knowledge of assets and how the investment cycle will proceed.

Strategize To Be Successful.

You need to know what you're bringing to the table. It will take a strong and independent plan to maintain it once the company is launched.

Understanding where to draw the line is also critical.

Always be careful when considering alternative liquid investments.

The director of the hedge fund must make informed decisions regarding licensed products and investment services. They need to be transparent as to whether the registered company is right for them and carefully consider the alternative liquid investment sector.

Your Best Friend Is Technology.

Startup Hedge fund manager chooses cloud-based solutions instead of conventional on-premise services. The benefits vary from cost containment to increased flexibility and IT management systems simplification.

Safety is the main concern here on the basis of IT or cloud. It is essential to protect the organization's data. In case of emergency, the hedge fund manager should also concentrate on disaster recovery plans.

Follow the Stock Gurus Success Mantra.

Whether you are seasoned investor or a newbie, if you're researching stock market gurus tactics from Warren Buffet to George Soros, you can make better investment decisions.

You may not receive a billion dollars a day or become an authoritative voice for the investing community, but you will learn to manage smart money. Here are some of the masters ' wisdom pearls...

HEDGE FUND FREQUENTLY ASKED QUESTIONS (FAQ)

What does starting a hedge fund cost?

There are a lot of costs to start a hedge fund. Normally a manager of the hedge fund will have to retain a lawyer, accountant and director of the hedge fund, as well as set up bank and brokerage accounts. All these relationships create costs for the manager of the hedge fund.

How long does a hedge fund start?

Basically, it will depend on how the director is trained and how efficiently the lawyer will function. It will also rely on whether the director has to be licensed as an investment advisor. In general, though, should a donor be able to get a fund up and running within 6-8 weeks if no registration is needed.

How many investors can I have in my fund and what sort of investors?

Two forms of hedge funds are available: 3(c)(1) and 3(c)(7). Up to 99 investors may have a 3(c)(1) hedge fund. Such investors will typically need to be "accredited investors," although some funds will choose to have as many as 35 non-accredited investors as possible. Such investors may usually also be "professional clients." Up to 499 "qualified clients" may have a 3(c)(7) hedge fund.

Can an IRA invest in the hedge fund?

Generally speaking, yes. Nevertheless, if a hedge fund wants to have IRA contributions, certain things should be addressed by the director with his lawyer.

Must a hedge fund manager be a certified investment consultant?

Generally, it will depend on the state of residence of the hedge fund manager. It can also depend on whether the fund exceeds the ERISA threshold of 25 percent.

Need a Series 7 license for a manager to run a Hedge Fund?

No. There is no requirement for a Series 7 exam license to manage a hedge fund. Nevertheless, if the hedge fund, or an associate, is licensed as a broker dealer, depending on his duties with the fund or affiliate, the director may need the Series 7.

To manage a Forex Hedge Fund, a manager needs a Series 7 license?

Typically no. Nevertheless, the manager may need to be licensed as a commodity pool operator depending on the nature of the forex hedge fund. If the director of the hedge fund was expected to be the principal's commodity pool operator and traders, a Series 3 exam license would be required.

How do investors find a hedge fund manager?

This is the million dollar hedge fund question. Typically, a hedge fund manager will look at friends and family and then the manager will attempt to raise capital from institutional investors (credit andrea) after an attractive track record is established. A hedge fund manager must ensure that he does not participate in any practices that may be considered public advertisement or solicitation in accordance with the rules of Regulation D.

Can a hedge fund have a website?

Sure, but that doesn't mean the hedge fund or director can use the internet to ask customers. The director will have to ensure that the website fulfills those criteria as stated in no-action letters from SEC.

What are the usual charges for the hedge fund?

Perhaps the most quoted fee structure is a 2 percent management fee and a 20 percent performance fee, but based on a variety of factors, including investment strategy and structure, each hedge fund will be different.

MANAGED FUTURES VS HEDGE FUNDS

For an alternative investment, are you on the market? If you are one of the conservative investors seeking to allocate a portion of the capital to approaches that are not commonly used by the buying public, this article is a must read.

There are two main forms of alternative investment management, hedge funds and futures managed. Hedge funds are invested in a wide range of products, both listed on exchange and derivatives Over - the-Counter (OTC). In general, controlled futures are only investments in contracts for exchange-listed commodity futures, governed by the Commodity Futures Trading Commission (CFTC). Be vigilant about it! The consumer can be left with a bad experience with alternative investment products if the wrong investment is selected. In relation to the alternative asset class, this section will concentrate on the very important issues of transparency, liquidity, lock-ups, returns and tax.

Transparency

With any investment, transparency is an issue. Many investors want to know at all times precisely what their money is doing. It's generally a bad idea to give money to someone who claims to have X returns without realizing what the agent is really doing. As the universe of investable products grows exponentially, transparency is becoming increasingly an issue. The latest "blow-ups" hedge fund is a case in point.

Hedge funds are alternative investment instruments that can be invested in anything from the common stock of Johnson and Johnson to Zimbabwe-based counter derivatives. The material universe is virtually unlimited. When an investor becomes a hedge fund's limited partner, he / she gives it free reign over the funds they've invested in most situations. If the director wants to do so, he

/ she might be able to invest in waffles and the shareholder would never have any idea. Hedge funds are not required to tell investors precisely where they are investing assets. To worsen the matters at the end of the day, many of the products don't have a closing value, so even if the investors knew what the funds were invested in, they wouldn't have any idea what their investment was worth on any given day. There is no accountability at all. All the investors get is a quarterly report that tells them about gains or losses and maybe a message if the director isn't too busy. In some cases, investors hear that more than 50% of their funds have been lost virtually overnight. Long-Term Capital Management is the most infamous case of a "blowing up" hedge fund, but a few more have recently gone down in history, the 30-40% loss of Absolute Capital Groups, and the 80% loss of Focus Capital in early 2008.

If the investor is involved in a managed futures product or with a Commodity Trading Advisor

(CTA), the story is much clearer. Generally speaking, a CTA has a very specific strategy outlined in the disclosure report of the investor which is similar to a prospectus. The CTA will state exactly in which goods the money of the investor will be invested as well as in exactly how the director wants to invest. What's more, each time a trade is made, a claim will be issued when traded with a CTA investor At the end of each day the products with a closing price determined by the exchange in which investor capital is deployed. This helps the investor to know exactly the value of his / her investment.

What makes him or her comfortable is really up to the investor. When one person does not know where his resources are invested then the question of accountability may not have to be discussed, but it is of the utmost importance for most of us.

Liquidity

Liquidity: a concept of trade, economics or

investment that refers to the ability of assets to be quickly transformed into money by an act of buying or selling without causing significant price movement and with minimal value loss. (Defined by wikipedia.org) Liquidity may be a concern with both hedge funds and futures managed, but a good manager would tend to avoid securities that are illiquid or difficult to trade in and out.

As mentioned earlier, managers of hedge funds can and do invest in a wide range of products. Many of these commodities are directly traded between banks and hedge funds as OTC derivatives or products. If the hedge fund buys an OTC derivative from a bank, and later decides that it needs to sell back that particular product, the bank alone will determine what to buy it back for, or worse, if they can buy it back for anything. Hedge fund may not be able to recover from a losing position in that scenario.

Liquidity is a question that has recently taken hold of a variety of hedge funds. Many were forced to shut down for investing in highly illiquid derivatives linked to subprime mortgages. When the counterparties started refusing to buy back the goods, the funds had no choice but to liquidate their investments at extremely discounted prices and close their doors or deny requests from investors to withdraw their money.

Liquidity can also be a problem for controlled futures, sadly. Most managers deal only in highly liquid commodities, but there are periods when even the most liquid commodities can very easily become illiquid. Multiple factors may cause illiquidity, from economics to supply and demand imbalances to fear and covetousness of general investors. A wise director can prevent investors being too vulnerable to liquidity risks by introducing some kind of account protection, diversification, or appropriate position sizing.

The counterparty to any exchange typically has a range of other counterparties willing to buy or sell at agreed rates while trading in listed markets, as do most regulated futures products. In general, this kind of open auction system allows for fair prices. Each account is guaranteed by the exchange clearing house through customer margin deposits to give investors even more comfort, meaning that the chance of a defaulting counterparty on any transaction is drastically reduced. Nevertheless, when dealing with obscure OTC markets, as many hedge funds do, most of the time there is only one equivalent to trade, meaning it is not guaranteed by anyone, which not only increases the chance of default, but also reduces the likelihood of a fair price for any exchange.

It is good to understand how volatility can affect the investment when investing in a hedge fund or managed futures product. If a company uses too much leverage or is regularly interested in less liquid thinly traded OTC goods, it may be an indication that it is not prudent at that time to invest in that asset.

Lock Up Period

A lock-up period is the time after the initial investment that does not allow the investor to withdraw funds from that particular vehicle. After the specified period of lock-up investors are free to withdraw funds as defined in each hedge fund's disclosure document.

There is a lock-up period for almost all hedge funds. This can vary from as little as three months to more than two years. Generally, the longer the lock-up duration, the more the fund has been created. In general, a lock-up period is good for managers and not so good for investors. If a manager has a one-year lock-up period and the trading begins to go poorly immediately after making an investment, that manager has the right to continue trading that money until the lock-up period has expired; because the investor has previously agreed to the terms and conditions in the disclosure document that he or she can not apply for redemption until the specified time period has expired.

Products handled in the future are different Most of the futures products managed do not have periods of lock-up. Some people have lock-ups ranging from three months to a year, but this is not the industry's status quo. If an investment needs to be redeemed in a managed futures product, it can usually be taken care of within a few hours. This is very beneficial if you have to pay taxes, college tuition, or any unforeseen expenses that arise.

Lock-up periods will be alien to most investors that have not previously invested in alternative investments. Make sure the lock-up and withdrawal dates are adequately addressed when reviewing the disclosure file. Please remember that the lock-up period in many situations is an environment that can be resolved for the benefit of the shareholder.

Returns

Returns are returns, right? Right! Returns for any alternative investment are a very deceiving method of research. Most investors make investments based on past returns, but this is a theory that is flawed. The main issue is that there is absolutely nothing to do with past returns or future returns. This has been proved as once out-performing managers start to underperform and managers struggle to rise to the top. Wise investors are not going to base their investment decisions on past returns or future returns assumptions.

The truth is that no director really knows what annual returns will be. Managers can aim a certain return, but there is no guarantee of achieving the goal. Specifically, if any manager, whether hedge fund or CTA, promises a return that is a sign of seeking another manager. Likewise, if a director explores his / her past returns, it is a sign that he / she does not fully understand that returns are totally unrelated to each other and have no future impact.

Managers are able to post monthly returns and potential investors view them in numerous databases, but this is completely the wrong way to make any investment decision. Chasing returns leads investors down the wrong path and can affect their capital devastatingly (see "Transparency").

What investors need to do is search by technique, not by return, through these alternative investment managers. Upon reading about the market approach of the managers, the investor will pick a few advisors from each category. The investor will call each director until a few are determined and ask for more information and/or a meeting. All managers will have a disclosure document that can be given to potential investors and possibly some marketing material. It may be a difficult task to satisfy the director of a hedge fund unless the shareholder places a very large sum. Nonetheless, CTAs are usually much more open and willing to meet investors, so it is entirely possible to have a meeting with them.

When proper due diligence is completed and the shareholder likes the plan and approach of the director, it is possible to make an investment. Be cautious not to spend too many resources with any particular manager or style, as this is not properly diversified. Creating a portfolio of alternative asset managers across a wide range of approaches is smart for the investor, as this can reduce the risk of any particular manager or style.

Taxes

Hedge funds often provide very unfair tax treatment to investors because they are investing all over the world in many different products. This can probably have a wide range of effects on the total taxes of the shareholder. After each tax year, hedge funds disclose gains or losses of investors in August regularly, requiring an extension of filing. In fact, tax returns are very complicated, frequently over 30 pages for each fund in which they are invested. It could probably require a whole book to try and explain all the possible tax implications of a hedge fund. It is simply not possible to dive into the whole scope of hedge fund tax accounting at this point in time.

Tax accounting is very simple for managed futures products. Since most trades are conducted within the CFTC-regulated Regulated Futures Contracts (RFC), contracts are treated with the Internal Revenue Code Section 1256. In this case, 60% of profits will be taxed at the rate of long-term capital gains and 40% will be taxed at the rate of short-term capital gains. This effective tax rate of 23 percent offers a 12 percent advantage over hedge funds that trade regularly for a lucrative controlled futures product But in the case of large losses, this may be a stumbling block. When a loss is recorded and 60/40 treatment is chosen, the investor is allowed to carry forward only $3000 of those losses each year. This may be a real headache if the loss of the shareholder is large, because he / she can carry forward losses forever. There's a bright side to it, and that's when the investor created a portfolio of managed futures products and another manager made gains that the investor can write off the loss against that other manager's gains.

Ultimately, it is much simpler to calculate taxes for a managed futures product than for a hedge fund. This may not be a problem for some investors as their CPAs will manage everything, but it would be essential to consult with the CPA before investing in order to ensure that they are fully understand the implications of the new investment.

CONCLUSION

Hedge fund investment is a very good investment decision if all is carefully considered. Certain forms of mutual funds should also be considered that can potentially improve the market beating chances.

Higher risk typically means higher returns in the investment world. This is nowhere more true than the hedge fund world. Hedge funds can earn your money back multiple times over in a short time with high-risk investment strategies.

Yet hedge funds can also experience massive losses and failures that cost investors every dollar on the line they have. One reason so many rich people are investing in hedge funds is because they can afford to take on the risk, but it may not be true for you. You should fully invest in hedge funds if you are a new investor who meets accredited investor criteria. You might not want to, however.